LET'S EXPLORE SCIENCE

Make it Go

▲ David Evans and Claudette Williams ☐

DORLING KINDERSLEY, INC.

NEW YORK

A DORLING KINDERSLEY BOOK

Project Editors Dawn Sirett and Monica Byles
Art Editor Karen Fielding
Additional Design Gillian Allan and Nicki Simmonds
Managing Editor Jane Yorke
Managing Art Editor Chris Scollen
Production Jayne Wood
Photography by Paul Bricknell
U.S. Editor B. Alison Weir

First American Edition, 1992
10 9 8 7 6 5 4 3 2 1

Published in the United States by
Dorling Kindersley, Inc., 232 Madison Avenue
New York, New York 10016

ISBN: 1-56458-120-9

Library of Congress Cataloging-in-Publication Data
Evans, David, 1937–
   Make it go / David Evans & Claudette Williams. -- 1st American ed.
      p. cm. -- (Let's explore science)
   Includes index.
   Summary: Uses simple observations and experiments to explore the forces that
cause movement.
   ISBN 1-56458-120-9
   1. Force and energy--Experiments--Juvenile literature. [1. Force and
energy--Experiments. 2. Experiments.] I. Williams, Claudette. II. Title. III. Series.
QC73.4. E93 1992
531'.6--dc20   92-52816
                                                                       CIP
                                                                       AC

Reproduced by J. Film Process Singapore Pte., Ltd.
Printed and bound in Belgium by Proost

Dorling Kindersley would like to thank the following for their help in producing this
book: Susanna Price (for additional photography); Coral Mula (for safety symbol
artwork); Stella Love; Mark Richards; Roger Priddy; Chris Legee; Rowena Alsey;
Jane Coney; Julia Fletcher; Jenny Vaughan; Matthew Cooper; and the Futcher
School, Drayton, Portsmouth. Dorling Kindersley would also like to give special
thanks to the following for appearing in this book: Natalie Agada; Charlotte Brown;
Hannah Capleton; Gregory Coleman; Jake Gregory; Tony Locke; Jaime MacDonald;
Tanya Pham; Elizabeth Robert; Jay Sprake; Nadia Walters; and Charlie McCarthy.

Contents

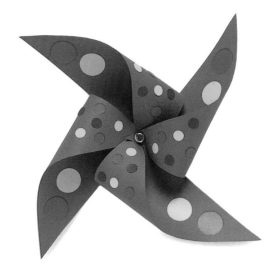

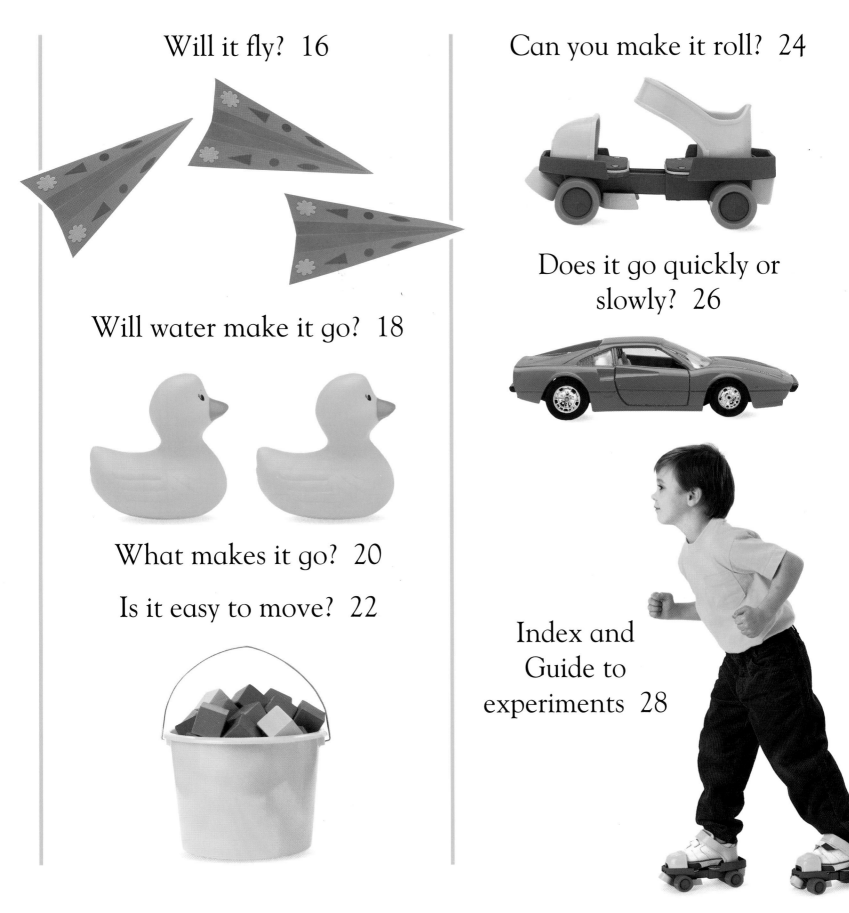

Note to parents and teachers

Young children are forever asking questions about the things they see, touch, hear, smell, and taste. The **Let's Explore Science** series aims to foster children's natural curiosity, and encourages them to use their senses to find out about science. Each book features a variety of experiments based on one topic, which draw on a young child's everyday experiences. By investigating familiar activities, such as bouncing a ball, making cakes, or clapping hands, young children will learn that science plays an important part in the world around them.

Investigative approach

Young children can only begin to understand science if they are stimulated to think and to find out for themselves. For these reasons, an open-ended questioning approach is used in the **Let's Explore Science** books and, wherever possible, results of experiments are not shown. Children are encouraged to make their own scientific discoveries, and to interpret them according to their own ideas. This investigative approach to learning makes science exciting and not just about acquiring "facts." It will assist children in many areas of their education.

Using the books

Before starting an experiment, check the text and pictures to ensure that you have gathered any necessary equipment. Allow children to help in this process and to suggest materials to use. Once ready, it is important to let children decide how to carry out the experiment and what the result means to them. You can help by asking questions, such as "What do you think will happen?" or "What did you do?"

Household equipment

All the experiments can be carried out easily at home. In most cases, inexpensive household objects and materials are used.

Guide to experiments

The *Guide to experiments* on pages 28-29 is intended to help parents, teachers, or helpers using this book with children. It gives an outline of the scientific principles underlying the experiments, includes useful tips for carrying out the activities, suggests alternative equipment to use, and additional activities to try.

Safe experimenting

This symbol appears next to experiments where children may require adult supervision or assistance, such as when they are heating things or using sharp tools.

About this book

Make it Go allows children to explore some of the basic principles associated with energy and forces. By finding various ways to make things go, children begin to learn about energy.

Energy is what makes things go or happen. It takes many forms, such as:

- potential energy (stored energy that can be released, for instance, when an object is dropped from a height);

- kinetic energy (the energy a body has when it is moving that can be transferred to another object);

- heat energy;

- electrical energy.

Energy can be converted from one form to another. For instance, when a ball rolls along a surface, it is subject to friction and some of the ball's kinetic energy is converted into other forms of energy, such as heat or sound.

Make it Go also allows children to investigate natural and manufactured forces. For instance, they make objects move by pushing or pulling them and use magnetic force to attract some metal objects.

With your help, young children will enjoy exploring the world of science and discover that finding out is fun.

David Evans and Claudette Williams

Can you go fast?

Try moving in different ways.
What can you do best?

Skipping
Can you skip with
a rope? What
happens when you
try to skip slowly?

Running
How fast
can you
run? Are you faster
or slower than your
friends?

Dancing
Can you dance slowly?
Can you dance quickly?
Which is easier to do?

Hopping

How fast can you hop on one leg? Can you hop faster on your other leg?

Jumping

Are you good at jumping? Can you jump quickly?

Spinning

Can you spin around quickly? What happens when you stand still after spinning?

Rolling

Can you do a forward roll? Can you roll fast?

Can you roll backward? Which is harder to do?

Can you make it go?

How can you make things move?
Are some ways easier than others?

Kicking
How far can
you kick a
ball? Can you
make the ball
go farther if
you throw it?

Bowling
How many pins can
you knock over with
one ball?

Heading
How long can you
keep a balloon in the
air, using your head?

Swinging

Can you make yourself go on a swing? How high can you go? When do you have to pull, and when do you have to push?

Pushing and pulling

Open and close a door. When do you have to push, and when do you have to pull?

Is it harder to push or pull a heavy cart?

Will air make it go?

Can you use air to make things go?

Hovercraft

Can you build a hovercraft? Ask an adult to cut a hole in a shoe box lid. Push a tube through the hole. What happens when you blow down the tube?

Pinwheel

How long can you keep a pinwheel's sails moving?

Paper fan

Can you use a fan to make sheets of paper move?

Blow football

Try playing blow football with a friend. How far does the ball move? What will happen when you both blow at the ball?

Wind racers

Have a blowing race with your friends. Push straws through pieces of cardboard to make sails. Use modeling clay to stick the sails onto toy cars. How fast can you make the cars go?

Will it fly?

How can you make things
fly through the air?

Kite
Can you keep
a kite in the air?
How high can
you make it go?

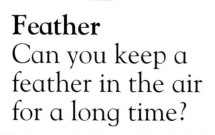

Feather
Can you keep a
feather in the air
for a long time?

Balloon
Blow up a balloon.
What will happen
when you let go?

Helicopter

Can you make a helicopter? Use a piece of thin cardboard. Cut and fold it like this and put a paper clip onto the middle flap.

Paper airplane

Can you make a plane fly quickly?

Skimmer

Can you skim a paper plate through the air? How far can you make it go?

Throw the helicopter up into the air. What happens?

17

Will water make it go?

Try these experiments and see if you
can use water to make things go.

Plastic plate

Can you move a plastic
plate with a jet of water
from a hose?

Boat

Can you make
a boat move by
splashing? Can
you make it go
forward and
then backward?

Rubber duck

Have a rubber duck race with a friend. Fill water pistols or plastic squeeze bottles with water. Can you make the ducks move quickly?

Waterwheel

Can you make a waterwheel, using a circle of thin cardboard and a pencil? Make cuts in the circle to form flaps.

Fold the flaps like this. Ask an adult to push a pencil through the middle of the cardboard. What happens when you pour water over the waterwheel?

What makes it go?

Try making different toys that go.

Bouncing bear
Attach a soft toy to a chain of rubber bands.

What happens when you pull on the toy and let go?

Spinning top
Ask an adult to help you make a spinning top with a circle of cardboard and a pencil. Can you make the top spin for a long time?

Magnet
Can you use a magnet to make things go?

spool

toothpick

rubber band

slice of candle

pencil

Twister

Can you make a twister? Thread a rubber band through a spool. Hold the band in place at one end with a piece of toothpick. Ask an adult to make a hole through the middle of a slice of candle. Thread the free end of the band through the candle slice. Then push a pencil through the band.

Wind up the rubber band, using the pencil to turn it. Put the twister on the floor.

What happens when you let go of the twister?

Is it easy to move?

Can you find different ways to make things move?

Spinning marble
Can you make a marble spin inside a plastic cup? Can you lift the cup off the floor without the marble falling out?

Heavy box
Ask a friend to sit in a box. Can you push your friend along?

Put broom handles under the box. What happens when you push your friend now?

loop of rope

spool

rope

Heavy bag
Do you find it easier to use your left hand or your right hand to lift a heavy bag?

Lever
Can you use a lever to lift a heavy box?

broom handle

block of wood

Heavy bucket
How high can you lift a heavy bucket? Make a pulley with some rope and a spool. Is it harder to lift the bucket using the pulley?

Try lifting the box by using a shorter lever. Is it easier?

Can you make it roll?

Try these experiments
to find out which things
roll the best.

On the floor
What rolls best
along the floor?

Along a track
Rest a toy track over a few
pillows to make a slope.

Which things roll best
along the track?

24

On a scooter

How far can you
go on a scooter?
Is it easier to go
up a slope or
down a slope?

On roller skates

Is it easier to
roller skate
on rough or
smooth ground?

On wheels

Do you have any toys
with wheels? Do the
toys roll best on a
flat surface or
on a slope?

Does it go quickly or slowly?

How can you change the speed
at which things go?

slope with matting

slope with carpet

smooth
slope

Down different slopes
Set up three slopes at the same
height. Cover two of them with
different materials.

What do you think will happen
when you roll the same object
down each slope?

In a tube

Can you make a marble
roll quickly in a tube?
How can you make
the marble roll
very slowly?

Down a
steep slope

Rest some toy
track on a
large box.
Roll some
marbles
down the
track.

Now rest the track on a
smaller box. Which slope
makes the marbles roll faster?

27

Index

Guide to experiments

The notes below briefly outline the scientific principles underlying the experiments and include suggestions for alternative equipment to use and activities to try.

Can you go fast? 10-11

Here children use their own bodies to explore basic principles associated with energy and forces. Ask them questions about the ways in which they can move, such as "Can you make large and small movements?" Try other activities, such as cartwheeling, walking, leaping, and crawling.

Can you make it go? 12-13

These experiments demonstrate to children that their own energy can be transferred to another object to make it go, such as when they kick a ball. Other activities children can try include bouncing a ball, flipping a coin, and playing with a yo-yo.

Will air make it go? 14-15

Here children investigate ways to transfer their own energy through the air by blowing and fanning. Ask children if they can control the way an object moves by blowing harder or more gently.

Will it fly? 16-17

By carrying out these experiments, children discover how they can make objects move through the air. You could develop the paper airplane activity by encouraging children to make planes of different sizes and from different types of paper. Ask them to find out which plane travels the greatest distance.

Will water make it go? 18-19

These experiments enable children to transfer their own energy through water to make things go. Encourage children to experiment with a powerful and a weak spurt of water. The waterwheel experiment will work just as well if you hold the waterwheel under a faucet.

What makes it go? 20-21

These experiments allow children to use magnets and a variety of other ways to make things move. The pulling force of the magnet attracts some metal objects, making them move. The rubber bands work as a kind of spring attached to the soft toy. Energy is stored when the rubber band is wound up inside the twister. Ask children what makes their own toys go. Encourage them to look at clockwork toys that are wound up and toys that have electric motors.

Is it easy to move? 22-23

Here children experiment with centrifugal force (when they spin a marble inside a cup) and discover that loads are easier to move when they use a lever, a pulley, or rollers (broom handles).

Can you make it roll? 24-25

Objects that roll overcome friction more efficiently. (Friction is generated when two materials come into contact and oppose one another.) Let children experiment with objects that will roll, others that will roll in an odd way, such as a cone, and some that will not roll at all.

Does it go quickly or slowly? 26-27

These activities introduce the idea of speed. The different surfaces on the slopes create varying amounts of friction, so the same object rolls at a different speed down each slope. The marble experiments show that changing the gradient of the slopes alters the rate at which the marbles can use their potential energy.

29

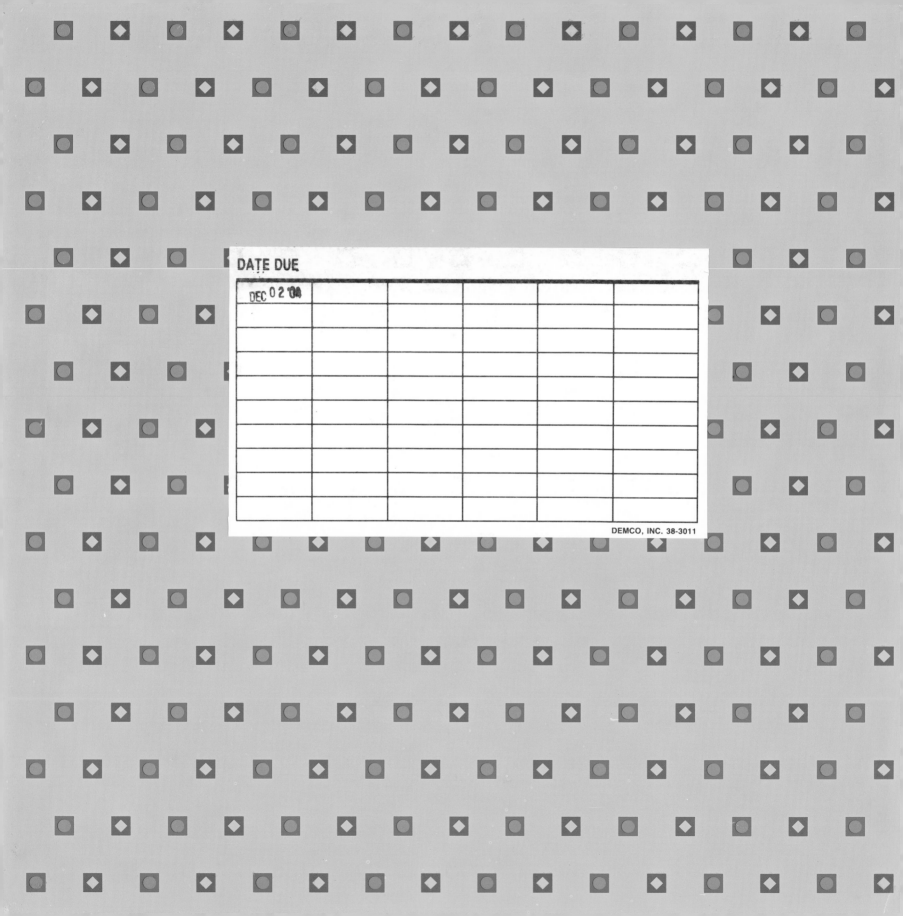

DATE DUE

DEC 02 '04					

DEMCO, INC. 38-3011